THE WI
CREATIVE
GUIDE TO

Cross Stitch

THE WI CREATIVE GUIDE TO

Cross Stitch

HILARY EVANS

UNWIN HYMAN

I would like to thank Elizabeth Nicholson and the WI for giving me the opportunity of seeing my own designs in print, my daughter Callie for her untiring help with the graphs and projects, Jane Elliot for her valuable editorial guidance and all the people who have helped in the stitching of my designs.

The publishers would like to thank DMC for kindly supplying the materials used in the book and the stitchers: Catherine, Caroline, Emma, Esther, Fenella, Jill, Kate, Sue, Wendy and Sophia.

For Callie

First published in Great Britain by Unwin Hyman, an imprint of Unwin Hyman Limited, 1987.

© Hilary Evans

UNWIN HYMAN LIMITED
Denmark House
37–39 Queen Elizabeth Street,
London SE1 2QB

and 40 Museum Street, London WC1A 1LU

Allen & Unwin Australia Pty Ltd
8 Napier Street, North Sydney, NSW 2060, Australia

Allen & Unwin New Zealand Pty Ltd with the Port Nicholson Press
60 Cambridge Terrace, Wellington, New Zealand

British Library Cataloguing in Publication Data
The WI creative guide to cross stitch.
1. Cross-stitch
I. Time II. National Federation of Women's Institutes
746.44   TT778.C76

ISBN 0 04 440062 4

Designed by Colin Lewis and Associates
Typeset by Latimer Trend & Company Ltd, Plymouth
Printed in Portugal by
Printer Portuguesa, Sintra

CONTENTS

INTRODUCTION

The origins of cross stitch can be traced far back in history appearing in the embroidery repertoires of many countries, from India and Persia to the peasant communities of South East Europe. In Britain flower motifs and samplers have been traditionally worked in cross stitch since the middle ages. Because of its durability cross stitch features frequently in ecclesiastical embroidery, particularly on hassocks where the lovingly worked designs would not be marred by generations of knees.

More recently cross stitch embroidery has been over-shadowed by tapestry (canvas work) but unjustly so as cross stitch is a charming and versatile form of embroidery. Simple to do it invariably produces a neat, professional and highly satisfying result. There are few tension problems as each cross is composed of two diagonal stitches which pull in opposite directions. Also the linen-type fabrics that the stitches are worked on are soft and pleasant to handle.

This book contains a selection of designs for pictures and motifs that can be embroidered onto table cloths, cushion covers or place mats. Either follow the suggestions or choose how you want to utilize the designs yourself. Instructions are not given on how to make the various items except for the greetings card (on page 96) as a very basic knowledge of needle work techniques is assumed. The graph for each design has its own colour code relating to DMC stranded cottons which have been used exclusively throughout the book.

I have tried to provide a varied and lively selection of subjects for cross-stitch embroidery. Obviously the choice of designs is highly personal but I hope that after a little practice you will be inspired to produce your own designs.

PART ONE

Simple

SIMPLE MOTIFS

All sizes are approximate.

Largest motif (star)

Design size: $2\frac{3}{4}$in, 7cm square

Fabric size: $4\frac{3}{4}$in, 12cm square for each motif

It is always satisfying to start with an easy project which is not expensive to produce but will give instant results. These simple shapes are the perfect introduction to cross stitch embroidery.

Uncomplicated motifs can be worked to make tiny pictures or attractive personalized greetings cards following the instructions in the Techniques Section (page 93). The heart is the easiest motif to sew and you can always leave out the shading stitches until you feel more confident.

One or several motifs can be worked as a repeat pattern to make a border and alternating rows of motifs look attractive on cushion covers. If you would like to work a selection of the motifs suggested or better still, your own designs, you could make a wall hanging by dividing a piece of fabric into squares with rows of horizontal and vertical stitches and working a single motif into each square producing a patchwork effect.

Before doing any stitching you have to find the centre of your fabric and the centre of the graph. This is all fully explained in the Techniques Section at the back of the book. Count the squares from the centre to the edge of the design and commence stitching. Use back stitch for the outline of the snowman.

824 ☑ 907 ◪ 996 ▨ 606 ⊡
893 ▨ 909 ▣ 310 ■ 552 ⊡

9

See instructions on page 12

WINDOWS

Design size: $3\frac{3}{4}$in, 10cm square

Fabric size: $6\frac{3}{4}$in, 17cm square for each window

Having experimented with the simple motifs you will have gained enough proficiency at cross stitching to tackle more ambitious windows. If you do not like the idea of the rainy day window, change it to a snow scene by leaving the cloud and snowflakes white (unstitched) and using the darker grey to fill in the background. Each window can be worked as a separate picture or the four could be grouped together in a line or as a square, leaving a gap of one inch between each square.

Find the centre of the fabric and the centre of the graph and stitch the window frame. Fill in the other details. Press and mount the picture as described in the Techniques Section ready for framing.

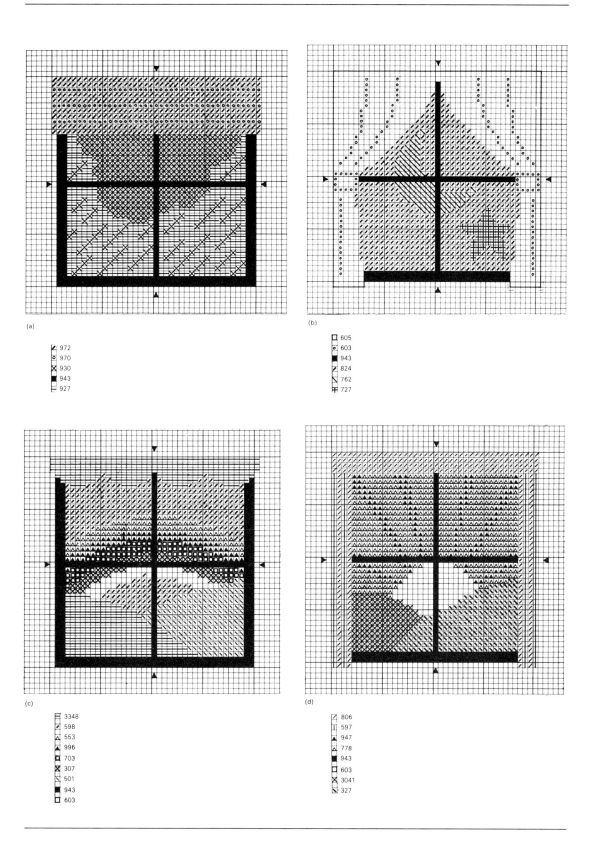

(a)

	972
	970
	930
	943
	927

(b)

	605
	603
	943
	824
	762
	727

(c)

	3348
	598
	553
	996
	703
	307
	501
	943
	603

(d)

	806
	597
	947
	778
	943
	603
	3041
	327

TOADSTOOLS

Design size: $4\frac{1}{2}$in, 15cm square

Fabric size: $7\frac{1}{2}$in, 19cm square for each design

I have always been fascinated by the strange shapes and colours of toadstools and mushrooms ever since I was taken for a walk in a damp, autumn wood as a child.

Apart from the magical quality of their fairy-tale appearance, the manner in which toadstools grow, springing up almost overnight, makes them particularly special. If there is a wood nearby, hunt through the areas of mossy carpet and around tree roots for your own examples.

Like the windows in the previous project the toadstools can be worked as separate pictures side by side allowing a gap of about half an inch between them.

Find the centre of the fabric and the centre of the graph and stitch the design. Press the finished embroidery and press ready for framing.

(a)

□	472
△	732
•	503
✕	3078
○	340
+	333
⊨	3046
╲	775
■	729
▫	645

(b)

■	754
▫	907
•	472
○	926
✕	350
⊞	606
⊨	3363
╲	928
▢	712
z	3011
ı	598

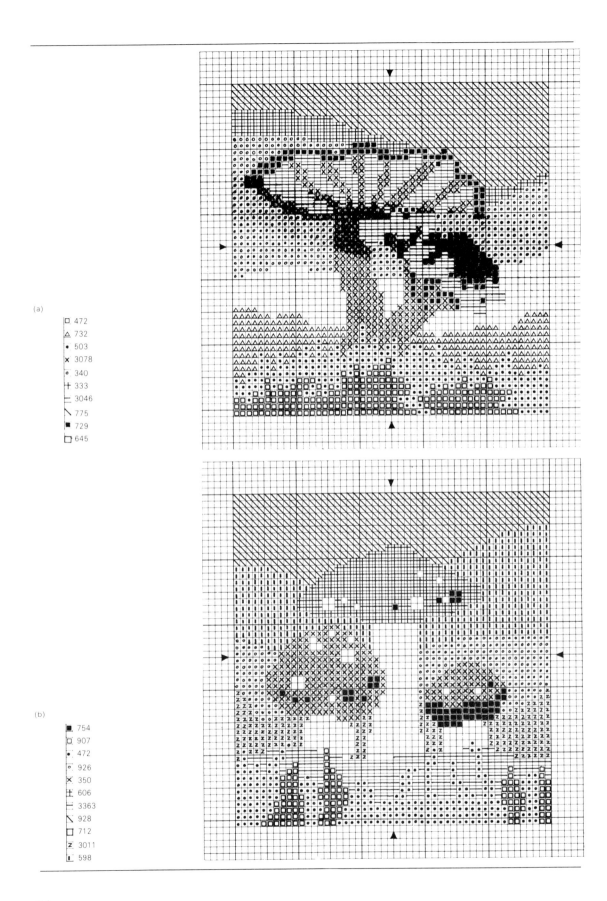

LANDSCAPE

Design size: $8\frac{1}{8}$in, 21cm $\times$ $6\frac{3}{4}$in, 17cm

Fabric size: 11in, 28cm $\times$ $9\frac{3}{4}$in, 25cm

This simple picture of hills and fields was inspired by the wonderful scenery of the dramatic Scottish countryside. Any landscape from craggy mountains to rolling hills or flat plains makes a perfect picture and complicated field systems will provide a patchwork of different blocks of colour in high summer. When designing your own landscape embroidery, observe the immense variety of greens produced by nature but ensure that when you choose the colours, the shades are not so subtle that they lose definition once worked. It is important to balance the colours correctly by choosing a good mixture of medium tones highlighted by light and dark ones.

Horizontal lines of stitches form the basis of this design making it easy to work and producing a quick result.

Find the centre of the fabric and the centre of the graph. Count the stitches to the top and edge of the design and commence stitching. Press and mount the finished design ready for framing.

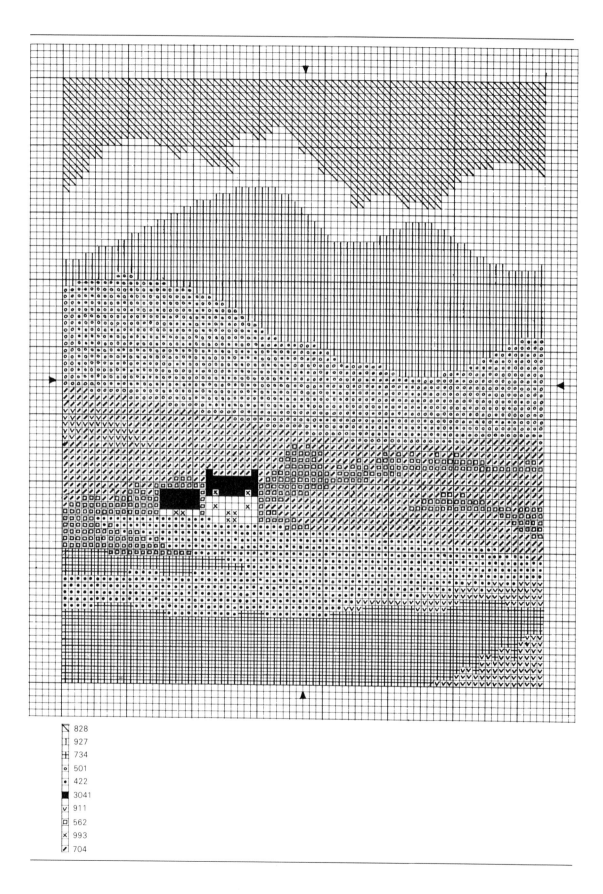

Symbol	Code
◺	828
Ⅱ	927
⌗	734
◌	501
•	422
■	3041
v	911
▫	562
x	993
◿	704

F I S H

Design size: 7in, 18cm × $6\frac{3}{4}$in, 17cm

Fabric size: 10in, 24cm × $9\frac{3}{4}$in, 25cm

It is easy to design an interesting picture of fish as they can be found in such an amazing variety of shapes and sizes. The colours vary from the soft muddy browns of river and deep sea fish to the steely silver of North Sea fish and the dazzling luminosity of tropical fish from coral reefs. For inspiration try the children's section of your local library as they often have good pictorial reference.

Make a large design of a single fish, observing its outline and individual markings or use several fish in a background of weeds, bubbles and wavy water lines. Do not attempt too much detail, just a few triangular shapes or zig-zag lines are adequate to represent the fish scales. Remember that most fish have dark backs and are light underneath.

Find the centre of the fabric and the centre of the graph. It is best to work this design from the top downwards. Press the finished embroidery and mount ready for framing.

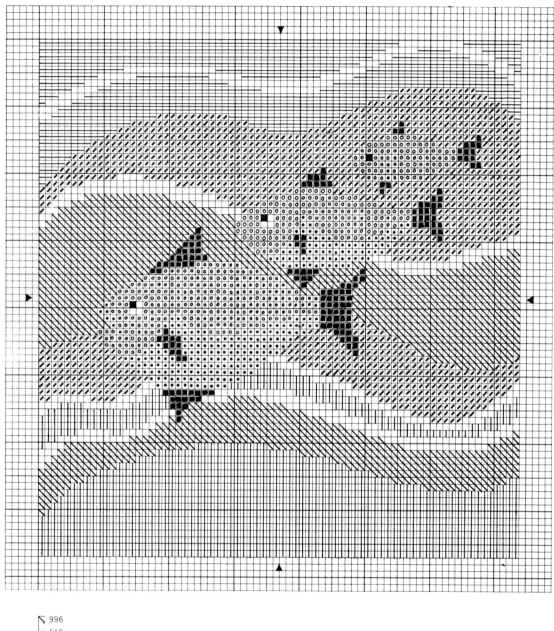

∇	996
⊢	519
⊥	797
⁄	943
▪	720
⦂	742
○	970
■	310

See instructions on page 24

TEAPOT

Design size: $7\frac{1}{2}$in, 19cm $\times$ $8\frac{3}{4}$in, 22cm

Fabric size: $11\frac{1}{2}$in, 29cm $\times$ $12\frac{3}{4}$in, 30.5cm for the picture

This design is perfect for a tea cozy, table cloth or a picture if you're the sort of person who loves a cup of tea! If blues and pinks don't appeal to you, change them to more subtle colours only remember that the teapot and cup need to be fairly strong so that they will stand out against a pale background.

Find the centre of the fabric and the centre of the graph and stitch the design. Press the finished embroidery and mount ready for framing. For the tea cozy cut two pieces of fabric to fit your teapot allowing a generous margin all round. Use the folding method to find the centre and embroider the design.

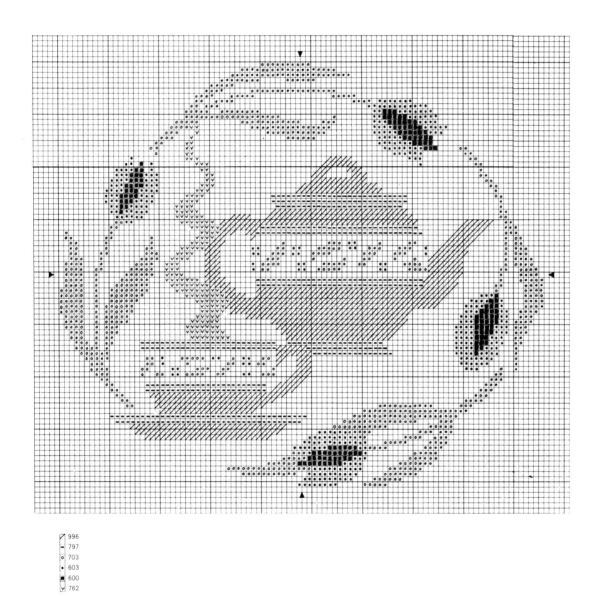

⚫	996
–	797
o	703
•	603
■	600
∨	762

WASHING LINE

Design size: $4\frac{1}{8}$in, 10.5cm $\times$ 9in, 23cm

Fabric size: 12in, 30cm $\times$ 16$\frac{1}{2}$in, 42cm for a place mat allowing $\frac{5}{8}$in, 1.5cm all round

A line of washing may seem rather dull upon first consideration probably because of its familiarity but I think the distorted shapes of clothes flapping about in a fairly lively breeze are very attractive. Try looking anew at everyday objects like kitchen utensils, cups and mugs; even a line of colourful plastic bottles from the bathroom would make an unusual but attractive picture.

This design can be worked as a repeating and alternating pattern around a table cloth or as a single design on a place mat. If you decide to work on a continuous pattern, omit the first clothes post from each adjoining line of washing. The posts can meet at right angles in the corners of the cloth avoiding any awkward diagonal stitching.

Before cutting fabric for a tablecloth, check how many pattern repeats will fit in (remembering to allow for borders and hems). For example—three pattern repeats will fit onto one square metre of fabric with a $\frac{3}{4}$in, 2cm border and 5in, 12.5cm hem allowance all round.

If you're embroidering one washing line on a place mat, decide if you want to centre the design or run it along the bottom or top edge. Find the centre of the fabric and the centre of the graph and stitch the design. Turn a $\frac{5}{8}$in, 1.5cm all round.

If you decide to run the design around a tablecloth calculate how many repeats will fit onto your fabric and stitch the posts in first and then fill in the rest of the pattern.

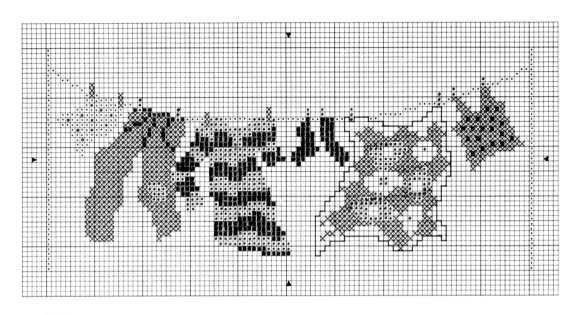

- ⊙ 892
- · 414
- ▪ 310
- ✕ 943

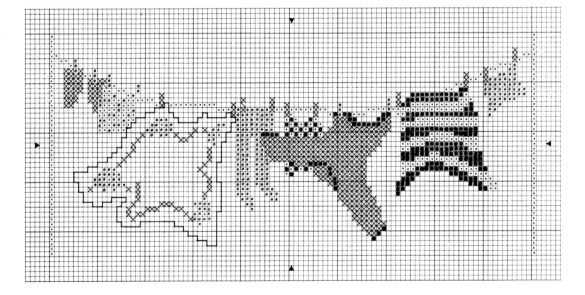

FLOWERS IN A VASE

Design size: $10\frac{3}{4}$in, 27cm × 7in, 18cm

Fabric size: $13\frac{3}{4}$in, 35cm × 10in, 25.5cm

There is a great tradition associated with floral cross stitch patterns, particularly in Denmark where needlewomen realized that the seemingly hard lines of cross stitch could be adapted most sympathetically to the graceful silhouettes of flowers. Flower subjects remain extremely popular and provide endless variety. Making a cross stitch picture of flowers is a lovely way of remembering a special bouquet, prize plant like an amarylis or the first spray of apple blossom and as a gift lasts longer than the real thing. If you have difficulty in drawing, make tracings from books and gardening magazines.

Find the centre of the fabric and the centre of the graph and stitch the design. Press and mount the finished embroidery ready for framing.

959	●	906	▥	945	I
747	╱	3348	✕	904	■
743	○	970	╲		

SEASIDE

This project is composed of three separate designs—Boats, Sandcastle and Prawns.

BOATS
Design size: $3\frac{1}{2}$in, 9cm × $6\frac{1}{2}$in, 16cm

Fabric size: $7\frac{1}{2}$in, 19cm × $10\frac{1}{2}$in, 26.5cm

SANDCASTLE
Design size: $4\frac{1}{4}$in, 11cm × 6in, 16.5cm

Fabric size: $8\frac{1}{4}$in, 21cm × $10\frac{1}{8}$in, 26cm

PRAWNS
Design size: $5\frac{1}{4}$in, 14cm × $8\frac{7}{8}$in, 22.5cm

Fabric size: $9\frac{1}{2}$in, 24cm × $12\frac{7}{8}$in, 33cm

These three motifs based on a seaside theme can be embroidered as pictures or stitched on a beach bag. You could stitch four repeats of the prawn design onto a square cushion reversing two of the motifs to give the impression of a cushion covered with pretty pink crustaceans!

The seaside provides wonderful scope for subject inspiration. Just consider the simple but pleasing shapes of beach huts, shells, deck chairs, yachts and windsurfers or more complicated forms of children playing, a pier, cliffs or rock pools. If you're still uninspired search through holiday snaps or travel brochures. Work your seaside designs in bright, sun-drenched colours or for more dramatic scenes in moody blues and greys.

For each motif find the centre of the fabric and the centre of the graph and stitch the design. Use backstitch for the prawns' feelers. Press the finished embroidery and mount ready for framing if appropriate.

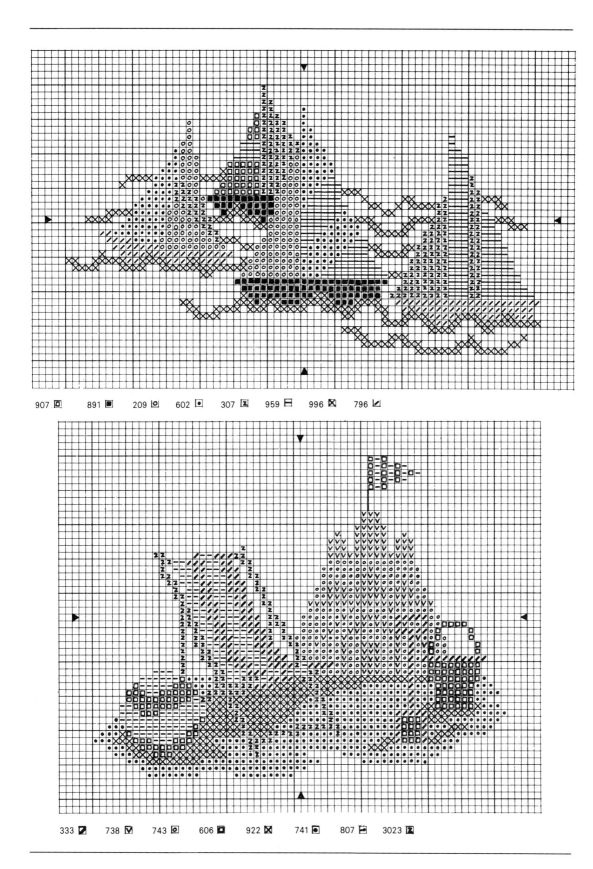

907 🔲   891 ◼   209 🔲   602 ⊡   307 ☒   959 ⊟   996 ☒   796 ◪

333 ◪   738 ☑   743 🔲   606 ◪   922 ☒   741 ◪   807 ⊟   3023 ☒

(a)

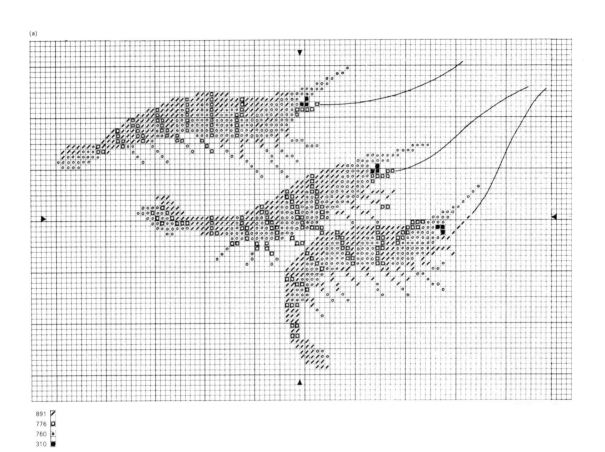

891 ◢
776 ▱
760 ◌
310 ◼

EGYPTIAN DESIGN

Design size: $8\frac{3}{4}$in, 22cm $\times$ $7\frac{1}{2}$in, 19cm

Fabric size: $11\frac{3}{4}$in, 30cm $\times$ $10\frac{1}{2}$in, 27cm

The ancient Egyptians were extremely accomplished artists, able to adapt complex forms to simple yet elegant designs and symbols. This particular design was inspired by a scarab charm pendant taken from the tomb of Tutankhamun. It was easy to convert to cross stitch due to its pure lines and distinct form.

The graph shows half the pattern as the design is symmetrical simply work the second half as a mirror image of the first.

Find the centre of the fabric and the centre of the graph and stitch the design. Press the finished embroidery and mount ready for framing.

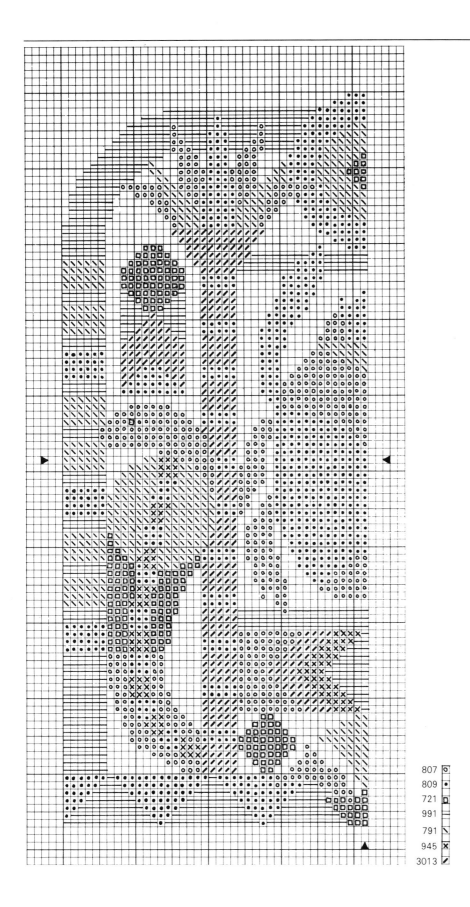

807	○
809	•
721	▢
991	▭
791	＼
945	✕
3013	／

38

PART TWO

Intermediate

MORNING GLORIES

Design size: $9\frac{3}{4}$in, 25cm × $7\frac{3}{8}$in, 19cm

Fabric size: $12\frac{3}{4}$in, 32cm × $10\frac{3}{8}$in, 26cm

Every spring I plant a pot of morning glory seeds and from June onwards throughout the summer these delicate climbing plants delight with a profusion of blue flowers. I designed this classic flower study to remind me of long summer days and clear, blue skies. Adapt the design so that it will fit into a different compositional field or separate out elements of the design to use as additional motifs if a larger area is to be decorated. Preferably, note the use of botanical form and create your own graph drawn from a favourite flower.

Find the centre of the fabric and the centre of the graph. Count the squares to the nearest stitch and embroider the design. Press the finished embroidery and mount ready for framing.

996 ⊡
987 ⊻
3347 ⊡
648 ■
703 ·
798 ⊠
445 ⊿

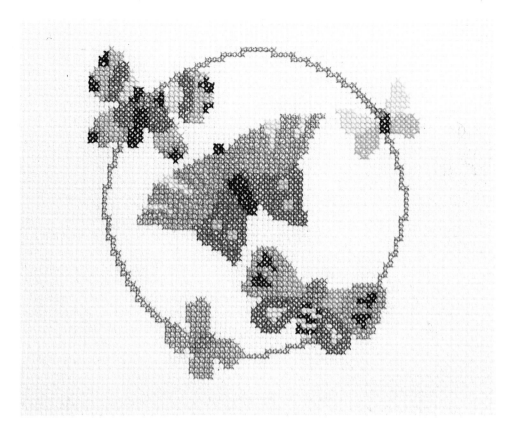

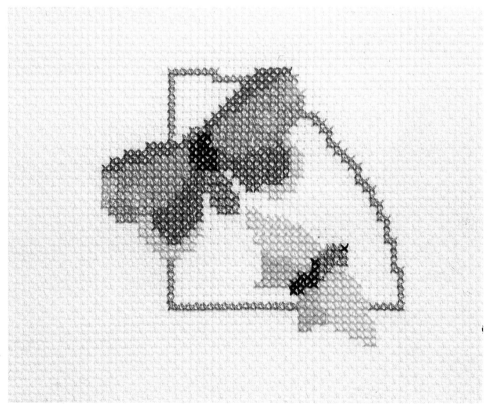

see instructions on page 44

BUTTERFLIES

Design size: 6in, 15cm square for circular motif
$3\frac{1}{2}$in, 9cm × $3\frac{7}{8}$in, 10cm for quarter circle motif

Fabric size: 10in, 25cm square for circular motif as a picture
17in, 43cm square for circular motif and quarter circular motifs
in each corner for a cushion cover (this includes a $\frac{7}{8}$in, 1.5cm
seam allowance all round)

Moths and butterflies are an exquisite source of inspiration.
Whether using the subtle, velvety shades of species indigen-
ous to Britain or the more flamboyant colouration of large
exotic butterflies—the effect is stunning.

The butterfly motifs here are suitable for a small tablecloth,
dressing table set or cushion cover. The circular motif can be
stitched as a picture. The quarter circle motif can be stitched in
corners, arranged to form a circle or used in alternating pairs
to form a scalloped edging design.

To make the picture or cushion cover, find the centre of the
fabric and the centre of the graph and stitch the design. Stitch
a quarter circle motif in each corner of the cushion cover
allowing a $1\frac{1}{2}$in, 4cm border all round. Press the finished
embroidery and mount ready for framing if appropriate.

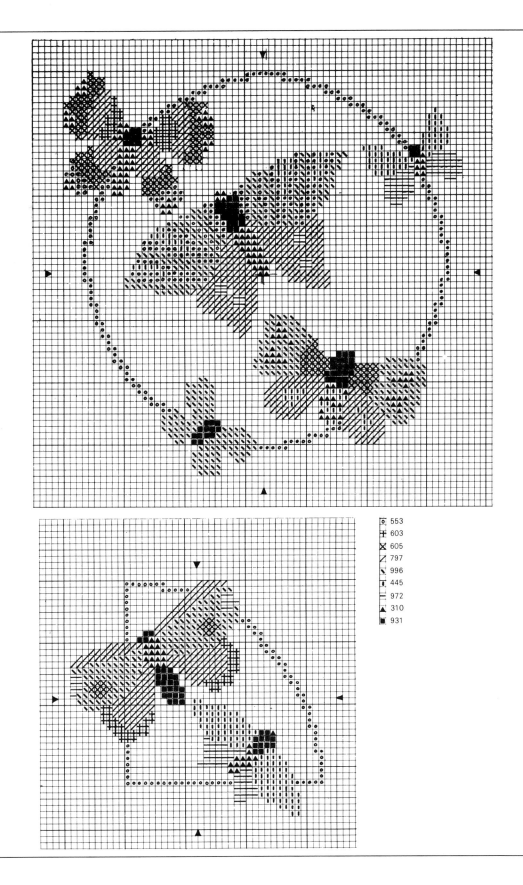

⊙	553
╫	603
✕	605
╱	797
╲	996
╥	445
═	972
▲	310
■	931

STRAWBERRIES

Design size: $9\frac{3}{4}$in, 25cm × $7\frac{3}{4}$in, 20cm for the large motif
4in, 10cm × $4\frac{1}{4}$in, 11cm for the small motif

Fabric size: 7in, 17.5cm × $7\frac{1}{4}$in, 28cm for small motif picture only

I encourage wild strawberries to spread all over my garden. Apart from enjoying the almost scented quality of the flavour of the fruit, the compact plants are very beautiful, especially when the first scarlet fruits appear alongside dainty white flowers. The familiar appearance of the seeds imbedded on the outside of the fruit makes a perfect conversion to cross stitch.

The two motifs can be embroidered in several combinations. The larger one can be repeated in reverse, forming a square to frame the small motif. A large motif can be embroidered in the corners of a tablecloth or the small motif could make a tiny picture. For a tablecloth embroider a large motif in each corner $1\frac{1}{2}$in, 4cm from the edges. This includes a $\frac{5}{8}$in, 1.5cm hem all round. For a picture using the small motif find the centre of the fabric and the centre of the graph and stitch the design. Press the finished embroidery and mount ready for framing.

973	■
891	○
701	▣
745	v
471	●
3052	✕
white	▢
321	▤

48

ICE CREAM SUNDAES

Design size: $6\frac{5}{8}$in, 17cm × 9in, 23cm

Fabric size: $9\frac{5}{8}$in, 24cm × 12in, 30cm

Some time ago when I was illustrating cookery books I made endless drawings of mushrooms, onions and peppers, (incidentally all of which are good cross stitch subjects) but I always wanted to illustrate luscious puddings and ice cream sundaes in particular, so I decided to embroider a design instead. Try designing a cross stitch picture of your favourite food, perhaps a colourful salad or a plate of eggs and bacon. Keep to definite, simple shapes as complicated forms are difficult to convert successfully.

Find the centre of the fabric and the centre of the graph and stitch the design. Press the finished embroidery and mount ready for framing.

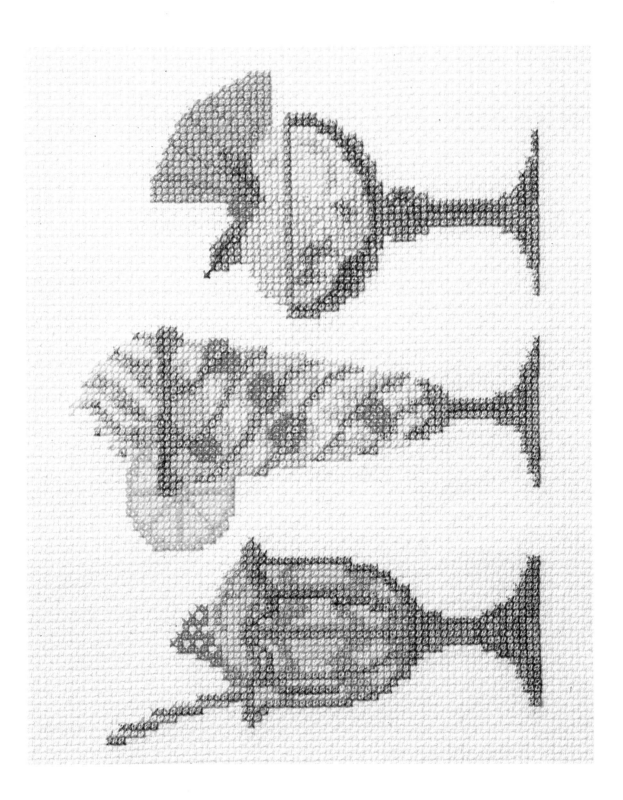

50

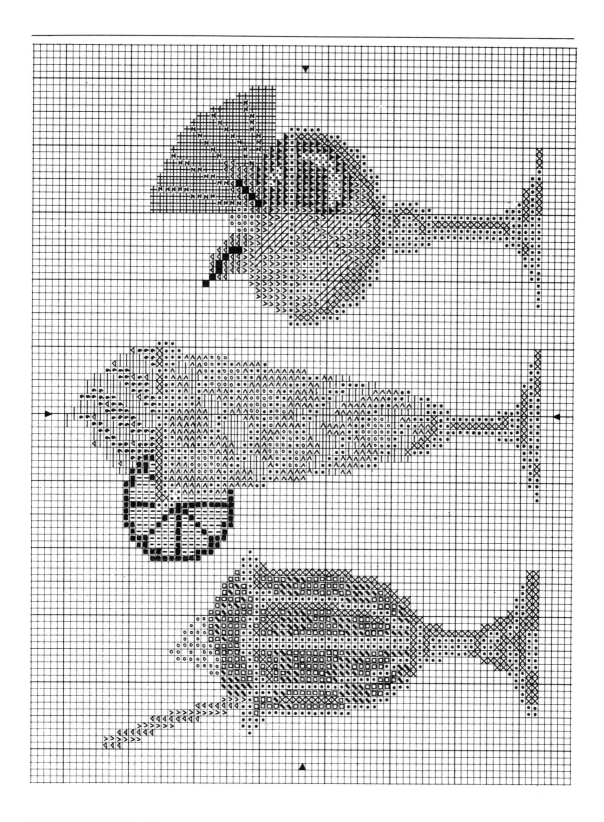

703 776 891 955 922 444 353 911 503 950 745 437 445 992 743 951 603 762

ORIENTAL PATTERN

Design size: $9\frac{1}{4}$in, 23.5cm × $7\frac{1}{2}$in, 19cm

Fabric size: $12\frac{1}{4}$in, 31cm × $10\frac{1}{2}$in, 27cm

I was thinking of the beautiful effect created by oriental carpets when I designed this pattern. Look in carpet shops for modern patterns to draw from, or research into any of the books on antique oriental carpets—the variety and scope of the woven designs is extraordinary.

Most geometric patterns can be worked out directly on graph paper using felt tip pens. The graph shows a quarter of the pattern.

Find the centre of the fabric and the centre of the graph and stitch the design. Press the finished embroidery and mount ready for framing.

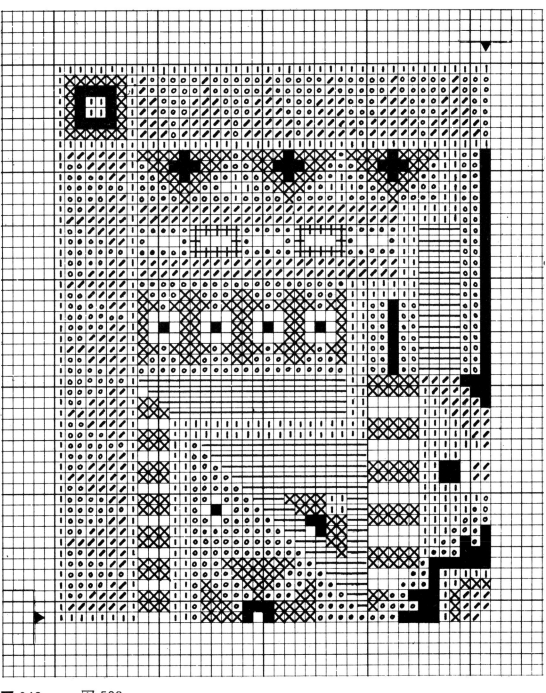

☐ 948	⫿ 500
☒ 353	⊟ 731
⧄ 612	■ 720
⊡ 958	

54

See instructions on page 56

TOUCAN

Design size: $9\frac{1}{4}$in, 23.5cm $\times$ $6\frac{3}{4}$in, 17cm including a $\frac{1}{2}$in, 1cm border at the top edge

Fabric size: $12\frac{1}{4}$in, 31cm $\times$ $9\frac{3}{4}$in, 25cm

You could brighten a dull corner with a picture of this comical Amazonian toucan. Its familiar and friendly face with striking colouration make it ideal for a child's bedroom or as a humorous note in your kitchen. Look at other exotic birds for stunning plumage, like the beautiful bird of paradise.

Find the centre of the fabric and the centre of the graph. Stitch the light and dark blue shading before filling in the black feathers. Press the finished embroidery and mount ready for framing.

Symbol	Color	Symbol	Color
■ 926		∨ 954	
▲ 959		⊥ 350	
△ 970		╫ 931	
• 310		↙ 905	
✕ 734		╤ 704	
° 610		◺ 311	
⊿ 830		▫ 743	

58

TAJ MAHAL

Design size: $8\frac{1}{8}$in, 20.5cm $\times$ $11\frac{3}{4}$in, 30cm this includes $\frac{3}{4}$in, 7mm border at the top of the design

Fabric size: $11\frac{1}{8}$in, 28cm $\times$ $14\frac{3}{4}$in, 37cm

The Taj Mahal is a wonderful piece of 17th-century Indian architecture built by an Emperor in memory of his wife. The building is renown for its romance and grandeur but all forms or architecture, whether monumental or humble, can be used as excellent studies for cross stitch patterns.

Even if you find drawing difficult you should be able to design a picture of your house or favourite building on graph paper. Using a soft pencil, start with the basic rectangular shape and add doors, windows and chimneys, gradually building up detail. When you are satisfied with the design, colour in the squares with felt tip pens.

Find the centre of the fabric and the centre of the graph and stitch the design. Press the finished embroidery and mount ready for framing.

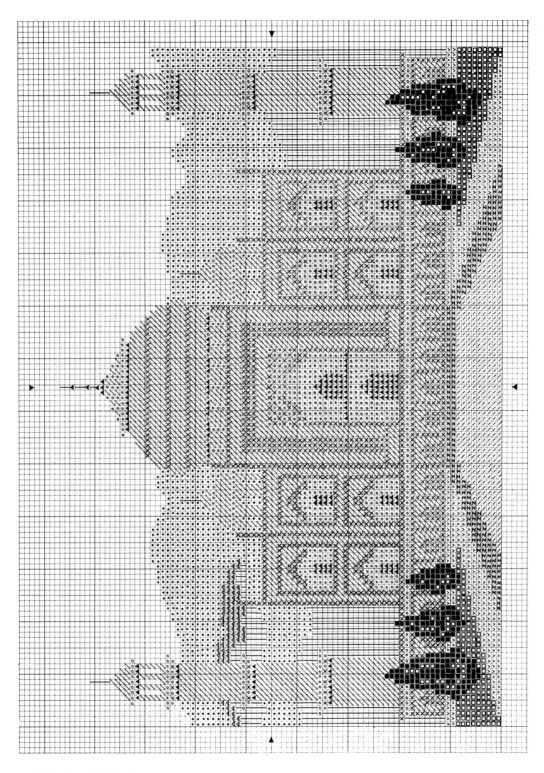

500
937
322
809
824
827
712
818
931
930
807
948

PALM TREE SUNSET

Design size: $8\frac{1}{4}$in, 21cm × 7in, 18cm

Fabric size: $11\frac{1}{4}$in, 28.5cm × 10in, 25cm

Whilst browsing through a travel brochure I found a photo-graph of this dramatic sunset. Look through holiday snaps, brochures or books for similar scenes. Only by analysing the colours for use in your design will you truly appreciate the vast spectrum covered by this natural event.

Find the centre of the fabric and the centre of the graph and stitch the design. Press the finished embroidery and mount ready for framing.

603
605
754
3341
818
315
351
310

The following patterns are more advanced; the forms are intricate to work and the colours used more numerous. By this stage you will be able to create and work sophisticated designs of your own, or alter the patterns given here, to reflect personal interests or observations. Do not feel you must slavishly follow the graphs – use your own ideas to extend motifs or experiment with entirely different colours.

PART THREE

Complicated

POTTED PLANTS
ON A WINDOW SILL

Design size: $6\frac{1}{4}$in, 16cm $\times$ $9\frac{7}{8}$in

Fabric size: $9\frac{1}{4}$in, 23.5cm $\times$ $12\frac{7}{8}$in, 51cm

Everyday objects provide an often surprising source of ideas and you will find yourself looking at the familiar things around you in a new light. These potted plants on my window sill struck me as being ideal for a cross-stitch embroidery.

Find the centre of the fabric and the centre of the graph and stitch the design. Press the finished embroidery and mount ready for framing.

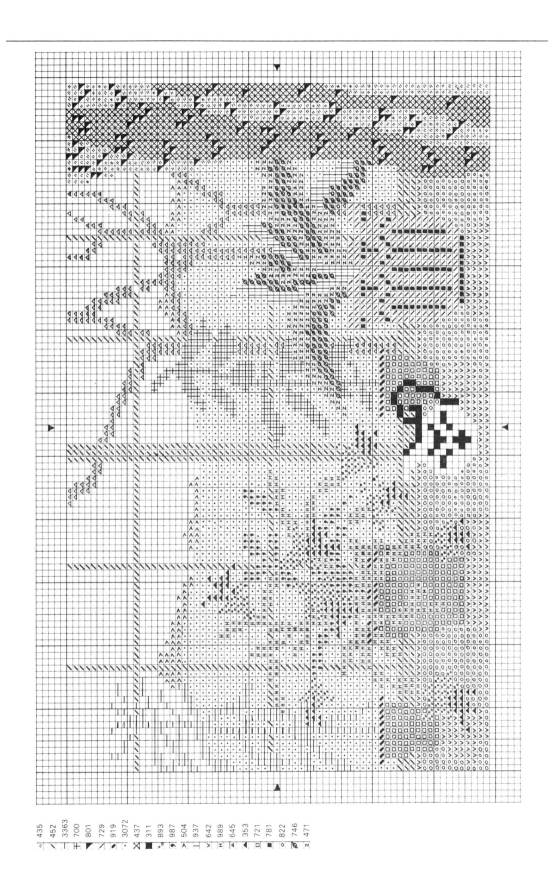

435
452
3363
700
801
729
919
3072
437
311
893
987
504
937
642
989
645
353
721
781
822
746
471

GIRL IN SWEATER

Design size: $8\frac{3}{4}$in, 22cm × $6\frac{3}{4}$in, 16.5cm this includes $\frac{3}{8}$in, 1cm border at the top of design

Fabric size: $11\frac{3}{4}$in, 30cm × $9\frac{3}{8}$in, 25cm

I rarely use figures in my pictures, preferring flowers and inanimate objects but I liked especially the pattern of the girl's sweater. Look through your photograph album and embroider a portrait of a member of your family. It's difficult to achieve an exact likeness so emphasize any distinguishing characteristics like large eyes, a moustache or rosy cheeks.

Find the centre of the fabric and the centre of the graph and stitch the design. Use back stitch to embroider the face. Press the finished embroidery and mount ready for framing.

○	792	■	598
▯	370		992
✖	3371	v	208
╱	869	•	3078
▮	733	▢	991
▢	948		

C A T

Design size: $9\frac{3}{4}$in, 25cm $\times$ $7\frac{1}{2}$in, 19cm including a $\frac{3}{4}$in, 6mm border on the right hand side, a $\frac{3}{16}$in, 5mm border on the left hand side and $\frac{7}{8}$in, 1in border top and bottom

Fabric size: $12\frac{3}{4}$in, 32cm $\times$ $10\frac{1}{2}$in, 27cm

Try creating a cross stitch portrait of your pet. Make working drawings, ideally from life if it will remain still for long enough or from photographs, before you embark on your design. Emphasize physical characteristics but include, if possible, any habits or preferences which make it so typically yours or your family's.

Find the centre of the fabric and the centre of the graph and stitch the design. Press the finished embroidery and mount ready for framing.

721	v	964	△
972	•	353	▲
400	◦	945	–
806	■	3012	╱

74

See instructions on page 76

CITYSCAPE

Design size: $6\frac{1}{4}$in, 16cm × $10\frac{1}{8}$in, 26cm includes $\frac{1}{2}$in, 1.5cm border at the top

Fabric size: $9\frac{1}{4}$in, 23.5cm × $13\frac{1}{8}$in, 33.5cm

In contrast to the flowing lines of landscapes, cityscapes are composed of sharp rectangular blocks of colour. The clear linear definition and solidity of the buildings create marvellous silhouettes which convert excellently into cross stitch designs.

Find the centre of the fabric and the centre of the graph and stitch the design. Press the finished embroidery and mount ready for framing.

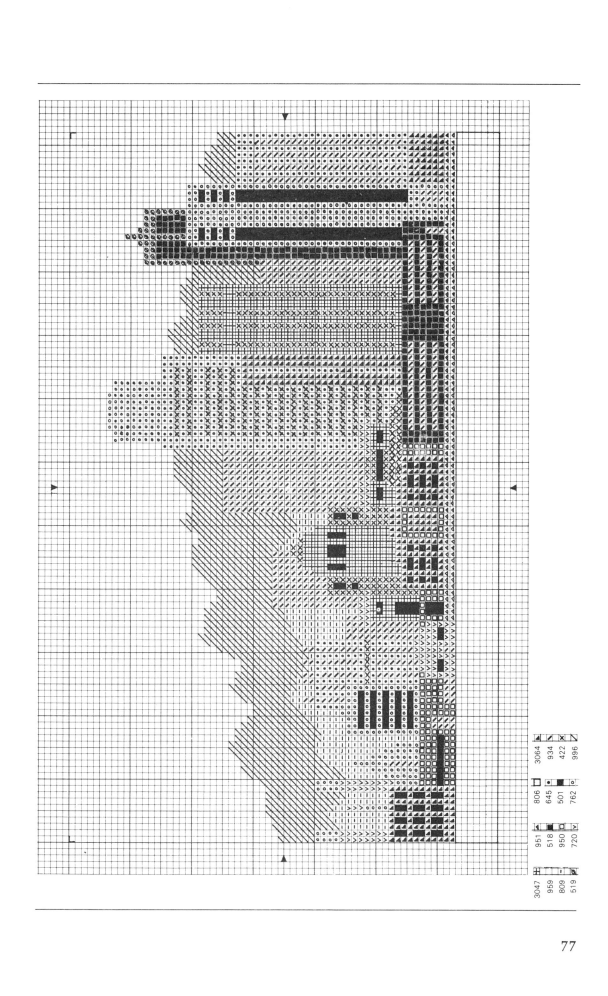

3064	◢	934	◿	422	⊠	996	◺

806	☐	645	⊡	501	■	762	⊙

951	◩	518	▣	950	▢	720	⊻

3047	⊞	959	⫿	809	⎯	519	◲

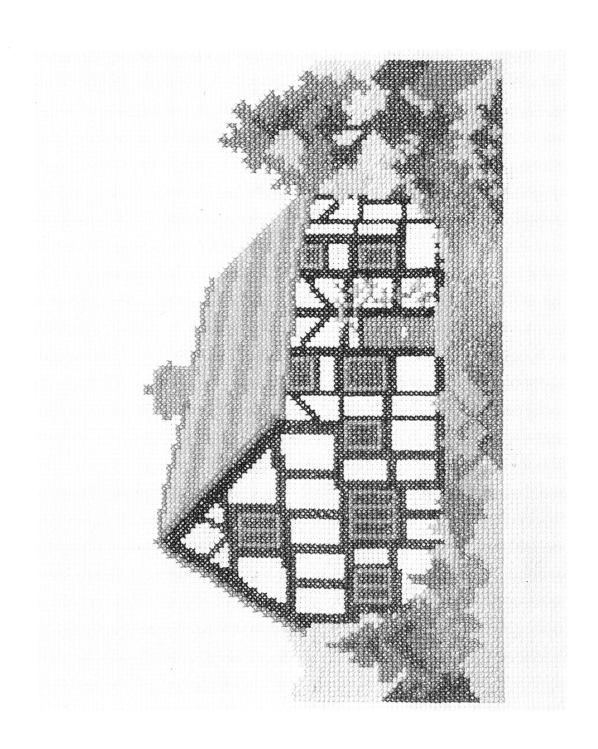

78

COTTAGE

Design size: $7\frac{1}{4}$in, 18.5cm × $11\frac{3}{4}$in, 30cm includes a $\frac{1}{2}$in, 1.3cm border at the top

Fabric size: $10\frac{1}{4}$in, 26cm × $14\frac{3}{4}$in, 37cm

An ever-popular theme, the country cottage will always make a charming picture. Note the gentle, curving lines which are so typical of vernacular architecture and take full advantage of the wonderful blooms which are so much a part of the established country gardens.

Find the centre of the fabric and the centre of the graph and stitch the design. Press the finished embroidery and mount ready for framing.

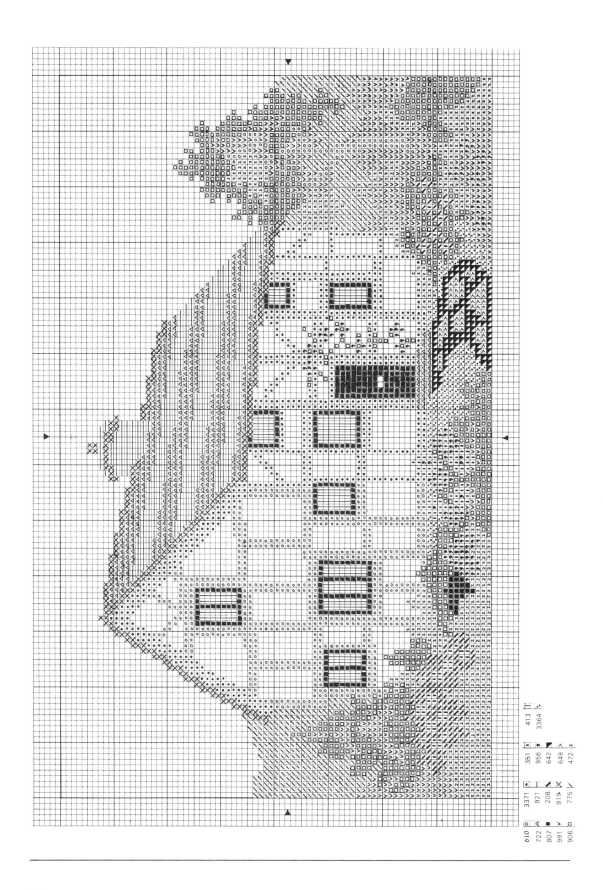

TREES

Design size: $9\frac{7}{8}$in, 25cm × $6\frac{1}{2}$in, 16.5cm

Fabric size: $12\frac{7}{8}$in, 33cm × $9\frac{1}{2}$in, 24cm

I use my camera to record sights that interest me and while walking through the beautiful grounds of Blenheim Palace one winter, I took several photos of trees and used them later as inspiration for this picture.

Find the centre of the fabric and the centre of the graph and stitch design. Press the finished embroidery and mount ready for framing.

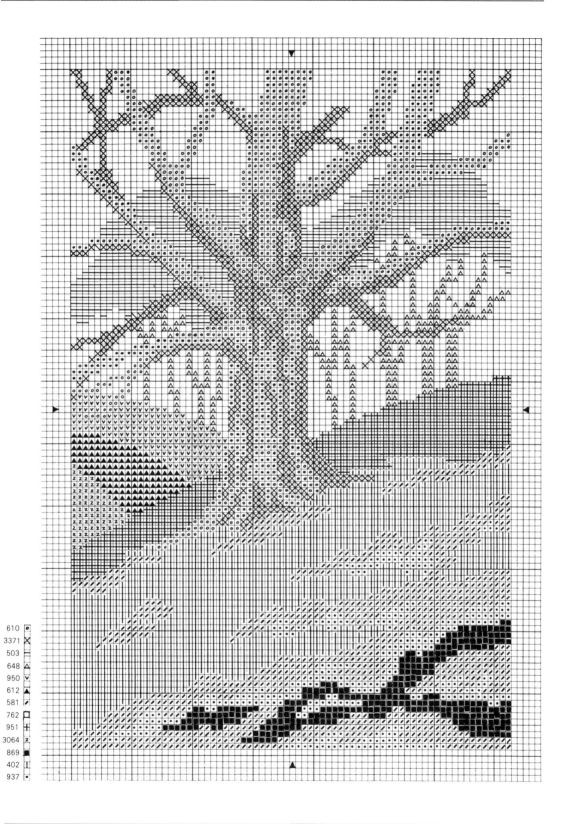

610	●
3371	✕
503	⊟
648	△
950	v
612	▲
581	◢
762	☐
951	⊞
3064	z
869	■
402	Ⅱ
937	•

GEESE

Design size: $8\frac{1}{4}$in, 21cm square

Fabric size: $11\frac{1}{4}$in, 29cm square

Geese are comical birds but they can be a little intimidating if they are annoyed. They will put their heads down and run at you hissing aggressively. Work this picture of three good tempered, if rather solemn geese on a fabric square as circular frames can be expensive and difficult to obtain.

Find the centre of the fabric and the centre of the graph and stitch the design. Press the finished embroidery and mount ready for framing.

310	■	451	◥
747	∖	523	▾
905	✕	722	○
3364	∨	453	z
772	•	3023	△
500	T	922	✛
945	⊢	611	⌐
971	▢		
743	z		
746			

See instructions on page 88

GREENHOUSE

Design size: $9\frac{7}{8}$in, 25cm × $6\frac{5}{8}$in, 17cm including $\frac{3}{16}$in, 5mm border at the sides and $\frac{1}{4}$in, 7mm border at the top and bottom

Fabric size: $12\frac{7}{8}$in, 33cm × $9\frac{7}{8}$in, 14cm

One of my favourite environments is inside a greenhouse on a windy, sunny day. I love the earthy smell and profusion of delicate plants quietly growing in the seclusion of their warm damp world. But you need not be a keen gardener to enjoy stitching this picture—as the contrast of glass and foliage is a visual treat if nothing more.

Find the centre of the fabric and the centre of the graph and stitch design. Press the finished embroidery and mount ready for framing.

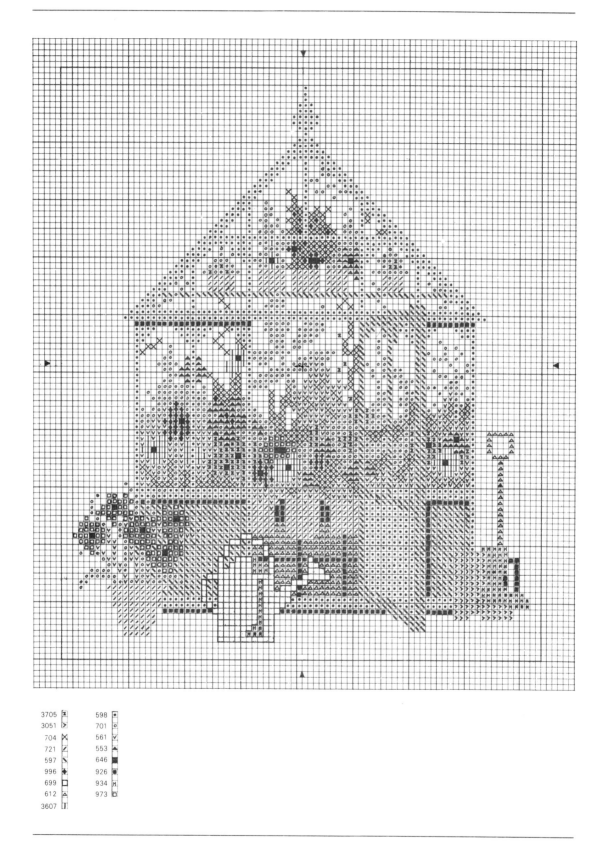

3705	Z	598	•
3051	⊵	701	○
704	✕	561	V
721	∕	553	▲
597	⟍	646	■
996	✦	926	▣
699	☐	934	Ħ
612	△	973	⊡
3607	⨿		

FLOWERS

Design size: $10\frac{1}{8}$in, 26cm × $7\frac{1}{4}$in, 18.5cm including frame

Fabric size: $13\frac{1}{8}$in, 33cm × $10\frac{1}{4}$in, 26cm

As I have already suggested, flowers provide an unending source of inspiration for design—the humblest weed is delightful when considered anew and the more dramatic hot house blooms can border on the fantastic.

You can stitch this flower composition with a dark background or you can omit the frame and background altogether for a lighter appearance.

Find the centre of the fabric and the centre of the graph and stitch the design. Press the finished embroidery and mount ready for framing.

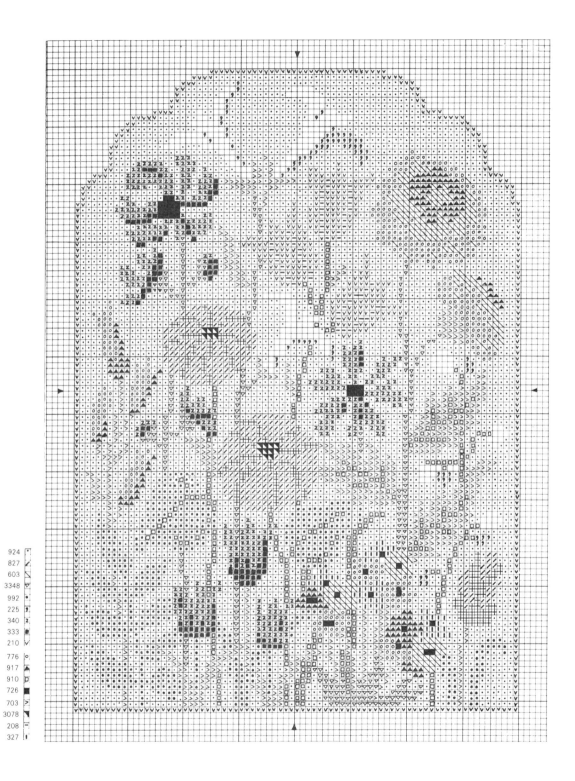

924	⬚
827	◢
603	◺
3348	▽
992	•
225	⁊
340	ᴢ
333	◼
210	⌄
776	◦
917	▲
910	◻
726	◼
703	▷
3078	◥
208	⁼
327	⫾

TECHNIQUES SECTION

FABRIC

Cross stitch can be worked on any linen-type evenweave fabric. That is one with warp and weft threads of even thickness. You must be able to count the individual threads but if you have visual difficulties, there are fabrics available where a number of threads are grouped closely together making the squares easily visible. You can use a woven fabric with uneven threads but the shape of the stitches will vary making them oblong shaped instead of square. An interesting free effect can be achieved by using a hessian fabric and a selection of threads e.g. wool, string, metallic thread, raffia etc.

All the designs in the book are worked on Pearl Aida Evenweave with a count of eleven stitches to the inch. Obviously finer threads will produce a smaller finished design. Remember to choose a fabric that is suitable for its finished purpose. Designs are usually worked on white or natural linen coloured fabrics but try using different colours and incorporate the background colour into the design. Note: before cross stitching oversew the edges of the fabric to prevent fraying.

THREADS

Stranded cotton thread is excellent for cross stitch embroidery as it can be divided according to the fabric to be embroidered. Throughout the book I have used two strands of DMC stranded cotton. A single strand would be suitable on fine linen and all six strands used as a single thread on a very coarse fabric.

There is a wonderful range of colours to choose from and you can always change the ones I have used for the designs to suit your particular task.

Twisted cotton and matt finish single threads are also available, so experiment with a range of threads and fabrics for different effects.

NEEDLES AND OTHER EQUIPMENT

Use blunt ended tapestry needles which are short but have a long eye. You will also need a small, sharp pair of scissors. You may find an embroidery hoop useful but it is not essential.

CROSS STITCH

Cross stitch is composed of two diagonal stitches worked over two threads. These can be stitched from left to right or right to left according to which feels more comfortable for you. All the top stitches should cross in the same direction.

 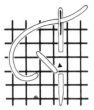

Stitches can be worked individually or in horizontal rows. Vertical and diagonal lines should be worked as separate stitches.

 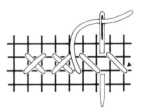

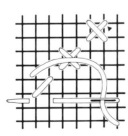 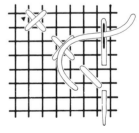

Keep the tension of the stitches as even as possible. Knots are bulky and show if the work is to be framed so leave a short length of thread that can be rethreaded and woven through several stitches at the back of the embroidery. Finish stitching in the same way and closely trim the ends of the thread.

BACK STITCH

Back stitch can be used when a shape needs defining or the design incorporates fine lines. Work the stitches over two threads.

PLACING THE DESIGN

To ensure that the design is placed centrally on the fabric, find the centre by folding the fabric in half and then in half again and mark the centre with a small safety pin. Find the centre of the graph by following the arrows at the edge until they meet in the middle. You can start stitching at the centre working downwards and outwards or you can count the rows of stitches to the top and edge of the design and commence stitching there. If there is no centre stitch on the graph count the threads to the nearest stitch. Try to keep the work as clean as possible.

PRESSING

When you have finished stitching, place the embroidery right side down on an ironing board and cover with a lightly dampened cloth. Press with a hot iron.

MOUNTING

Cut a piece of cardboard the same size as the design. Trim any surplus edging fabric if necessary.

Place the cardboard on the wrong side of the design, fold the sides over and secure with long zig-zag stitches. Fold the top and bottom edges over and secure likewise. Oversew the overlapping edges.

MAKING YOUR OWN GRAPHS

It is more satisfying to be able to embroider your own designs. Simple or geometric patterns can be worked directly onto graph paper using felt tip pens for the different colours. If you want to make designs from photographs or pictures in magazines first make a tracing. You may need to enlarge the design before drawing it on graph paper.

 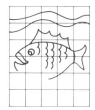

Divide the picture into squares and then redraw the design on another piece of tracing paper divided into the same number of larger squares. On the back of the tracing retrace the design using a soft lead pencil. Place the tracing on graph paper and using a hard pencil draw down the design. Remove the tracing and ink in the design on the graph paper matching the lines as closely as possible to the squares of the graph. The size of the design on the graph probably will not be the same as the finished embroidery, so work a small area first to calculate how much fabric you will need.

GREETINGS CARDS

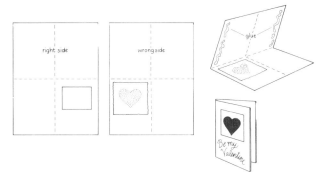

Fold a piece of stiff paper or thin card in half and half again. This will be the finished size of the greetings card. With the right side facing cut a shape to frame the embroidered motif in the bottom right hand quarter. Trim away any surplus fabric and glue the motif in place on the wrong side of the card. Glue the edges together.

SUPPLIES

All supplies used in this book should be available at large needlework stores. If you are having any difficulty in finding the DMC embroidery cotton and linen evenweave fabric write to Dunlicraft Ltd, Pullman Road, Wigston, Leicester LE8 2DY for information on local stockists.